How to Sell Houses without Selling Your Soul

Nationally Ranked Broker
Shares Her Path from
Part Time Agent to
Selling 250 Homes a Year

BECKY BABCOCK

Published by Babcock & Associates, Inc.

Printed by CreateSpace, An Amazon.com Company

Copyright © 2018 Becky Babcock

All rights reserved. No portion of this book may be used or reproduced, stored in a retrieval system, or transmitted in any form or by any means--electronic, mechanical, photocopy, recording, scanning or other--except for brief quotations embodied in critical reviews or articles, without the prior written permission of the publisher.

ISBN: 978-1986160018

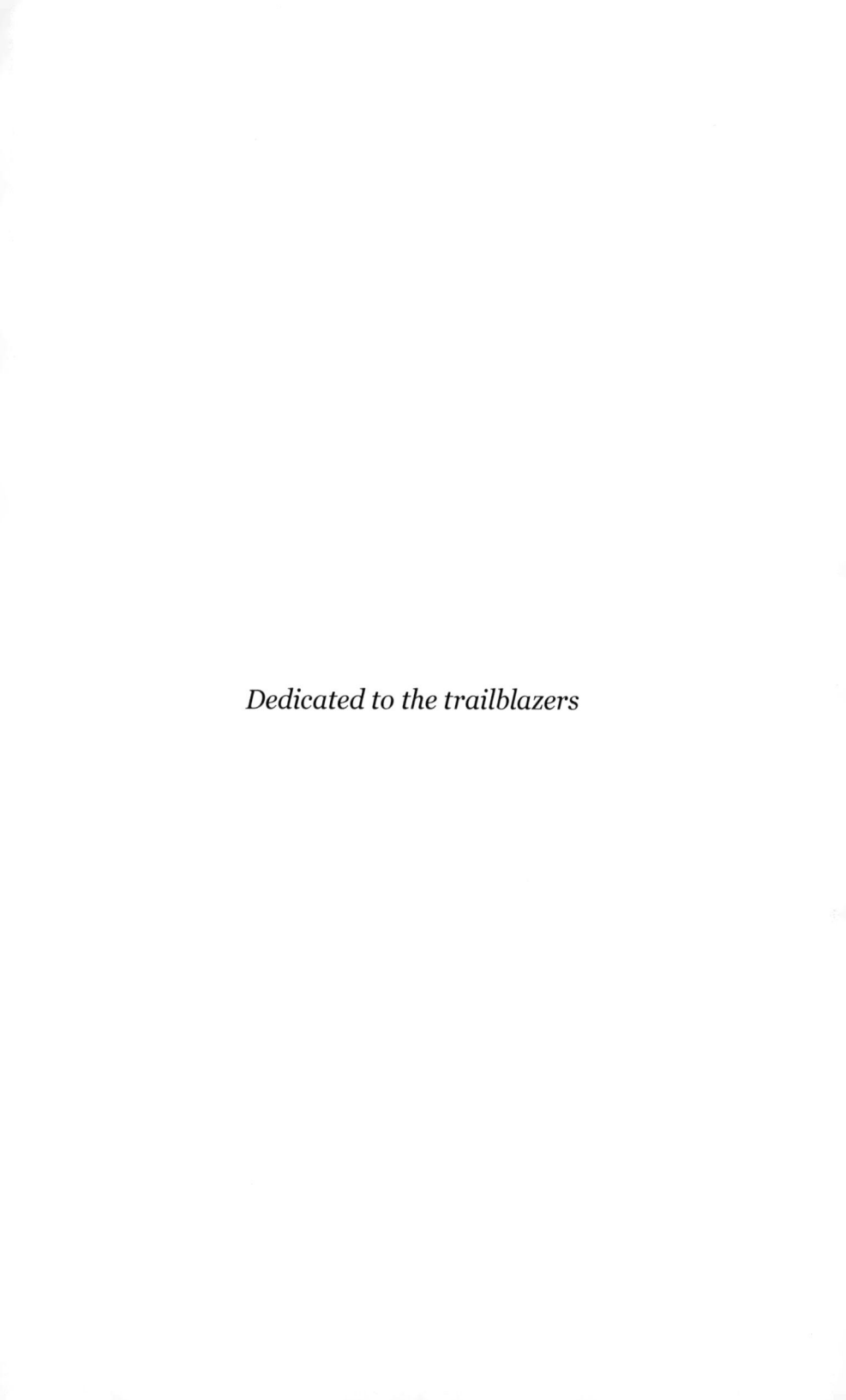

Dedicated to the trailblazers

CONTENTS

Acknowledgments — i
Forward — iii

FINDING MY PATH

1. Trust Your Intuition — 1
2. Find Your Passion And Make It Happen — 7
3. Home Is Where Community Is — 16
4. People Move For A Reason — 24
5. Life Transitions — 33
6. Sometimes A Path Finds You — 41

SHARING MY PATH

7. Find Colleagues Who Share Your Values — 56
8. Work On Your Business, Not Just In It — 64
9. Every Sale Has A Story — 75
10. What's In A Brand — 83
11. 11-12-13 — 97
12. Customize For Client Experiences — 104
13. Core Values — 111

Afterward: Path & Post — 115
About The Author — 119

ACKNOWLEDGMENTS

This book is dedicated to my life partner, best friend, and husband David. As childhood sweethearts, we began dating at 16, and married and bought our first home together at 19. We share the joys as well as the struggles of our lives, family, and careers – we make a great team. Without his constant support and cheering me on from the sidelines, I could never have found this path.

One thing I have learned over time is not to judge people based on their age. Sometimes people half our age have twice our skills. My daughter Michelle Babcock is someone like that. Without her tireless editing and pushing me to stay on track, I could never have gotten to the point of finishing this book. She is masterful at her craft of communicating, copy editing, and proofreading.

Growing up, my mom, Nyle Srok, was my greatest advocate and inspiration. She always worried about me being picked on for being the shortest one among her four children. So to compensate for my short stature, she made sure I was never raised to be a wallflower. She succeeded. :)

Finally, the culmination of this book marks the beginning of another story: The birth of Path & Post Real Estate couldn't have happened without my business partner and friend, Brad Nix. Our complementary strengths make us stronger and better as a team than as individuals. I look forward to doing great things together over the next decade as we grow our business.

To all the team members, agents, real estate leaders, friends, and family who have influenced, inspired, and supported me over the years, I thank you!

FORWARD

In 2013, my real estate team and I were at the peak of national real estate success. I was the number one agent in the U.S. in both sales and customer service for a national real estate franchise with more than 30,000 agents. That's when I decided to change everything by rebranding my team.

Everyone said, "If it isn't broke, don't fix it," but I believe if you aren't constantly shifting and innovating your business model to adapt to change in the market and culture, your business *will* break and you'll end up broke... pun intended.

So, while at the top of my game, I took my personal name out of the team name, changing everything else at the same time: website, brand, processes, and systems – everything.

Then, I changed it all again three years later when I opened an independent brokerage.

Some people are afraid of change; others are energized by it. Guess which one I am?

My story follows a crooked path with plenty of ups and downs, and lessons around each bend, as happens so often in life. Each person is a product of their life experiences, and sometimes our greatest lessons come from our toughest challenges – we can use those experiences to shape our future.

I started my real estate career as a solo agent and evolved into the leader of my award winning Becky Babcock Team, averaging up to 200 sales a year. But along with my success in real estate, I felt the crushing pressure of 80 hour work weeks and no time for life. After a decade of nonstop growth in my business, I reached a breaking point. The sheer volume of clients I was juggling took the joy out of my work – I felt like I was drowning, barely keeping my head above water.

Change was good for my team, but it didn't come easily. It required faith and perseverance, fueled by good, old fashioned hard work, intuition, and the guts to go against the status quo.

This is not a book to help you learn how to manipulate people into buying homes; there are plenty of sales books for that.

This is not a book to teach you the basic nuts and bolts of real estate; there are plenty of training seminars, books, coaches, and mentors to teach you that.

This book shares my story: it shows how rewarding your life and work can be if you are open to following your path, even when it takes unexpected turns, and sharing that path with others who align with your values and vision.

Hopefully you will find a few kernels of truth about marketing, branding, and leadership, but in a more relational way – not like a typical business sales book. You will find a focus on the influence of relationships, trust, and personality styles in business, and how those personality styles influence sales dynamics.

While some real estate mega teams are hyper-focused on the numbers, my team took the path less traveled by focusing on relationships and customer experiences – and the numbers have followed. As real estate agents, not only can we make a profit, we can also improve people's lives, and helping our clients is what gives meaning to our work. Focus on the reason and the results will follow.

FINDING MY PATH

1 TRUST YOUR INTUITION

I was too young to remember our family moving from place to place, but according to my mom, we moved six times in five years. We lived two places in California, two places in Texas, and one place in Maryland before settling in Georgia when I was 5 years old.

"If your father had an engineering degree, he wouldn't be stuck traveling. He would be able to have more input and say-so in his career path, and that's why it's important that you go to college, so you have more options," mom would say.

My father's job as a military contractor took him across the country to test jet engines. After several years of moving along with my dad as a family of six, including four young children, my parents decided to buy a home just north of Atlanta. My dad continued to travel for work and would come home every one or two weeks.

Because of his constant travel, my mom had to handle everything on her own: housework, cooking, homework help, after school activities, coaching sports... but their choice was either for our entire family to live as nomads, or find a place to grow roots and deal with the challenges of having one parent absent much of the time.

I grew up watching my mom take charge of everything in a time when women were expected to be exclusively housewives. Very few women worked in the 1970s, but my mom did. She baked bread, sewed clothes, and taught tennis lessons for money. She taught me by example to make my own path. My parents always wanted a big family, so in addition to me and my three siblings, my mom helped raise dozens of foster children, and worked for Cobb County Parks and Recreation – she was a busy woman!

Our family spent most weekends on the fields and courts at Shaw Park. The park was our second home. Nestled in a forest of trees, the fields were host to what seemed like an infinite number of sporting events. Bats cracking on baseballs and cheers from spectators came together to make a symphony of sports, and the smell of buttered popcorn from the concession stand permeated every corner of the park.

My siblings and I all played sports, and our mom was often our coach – softball, basketball, tennis. From as far back as I can remember, all the way through high school, I spent weekends at the park hanging out with my siblings and friends.

One afternoon I was home with my younger sister Julie, while Mom was at the park with our older brother Ed, and Dad was out of town for work. We got a phone call that Ed was being taken by ambulance to the hospital because he had an accident playing baseball.

He was covering first-base, and as Ed reached up to catch the ball, a runner put his head down and slammed into Ed's gut. My brother wrenched over in pain and mom ran out to the field to check on him. Later, I heard about the conversation that went on between my mom and the coach.

> "Come on Nyle, go sit down, I got your son, he'll be fine."
> "He's not fine."
> "Moms always overreact. He'll be fine!"

My mom's intuition was telling her something wasn't right. So she demanded Ed go to the emergency room. My mom called for an ambulance, despite the coach's disapproval and Ed's embarrassment. As the ambulance arrived, Ed passed out from what was later found to be a significant amount of internal blood loss.

I waited anxiously by the wall-mounted rotary phone with Julie, and would get periodic updates from the hospital. Mom called to tell us Ed was getting blood transfusions – he had turned white and didn't look good. I was 11 years old at the time; I was terrified.

He was losing blood, fast, and as a last-ditch effort to figure out what was wrong, a surgeon pressed on Ed's shoulder during an exam. From that seemingly obscure examination, the surgeon determined the pain was coming from Ed's spleen.

"Are you married?" The surgeon asked my mom. "It's time to call your husband home from New York, immediately."

My dad had to charter a private flight to get home. By that time, Ed had lost half of his blood. For 12 hours Ed was touch-and-go, and the doctors weren't sure if he would live.

That baseball injury the coach so readily downplayed as "a mother overreacting," had actually severed Ed's spleen – an injury that can easily be fatal.

If my mom hadn't followed her intuition, my brother would have bled to death at the park. She taught me the importance of trusting my instincts and choosing my own path.

Takeaways:
- Embrace your intuition
- Make your own path

2 FIND YOUR PASSION AND MAKE IT HAPPEN

My mom picked me up from tennis practice one day and said there was a young man who wanted to take me on a date.

"You're not supposed to date until you're 16, but your father and I have given him permission because he called and asked, and you're only two weeks away from being 16."
"It's David Babcock," mom said.
"That boy at the bus stop? Sure! I'll go!"

Our first date at the Saint Paul United Methodist Church's annual Christmas banquet led into years of dating, all through high school. A week and a half after graduation, David and I decided to get engaged. We agreed on a one-year engagement to give ourselves time to enroll in college, search for a starter house, and adjust to holidays with both sets of in-laws.

Despite our planning, the engagement worried my mom. When she was in college, it was said a married woman had no business going to school. My mom had lost her four-year academic scholarship for refusing to sign an agreement not to marry in college, so she worried I wouldn't finish a degree if I got married at 19.

But I had already made my mind up; I was determined to earn a college degree, to have control over my career, and to be married to the love of my life. I wanted a family and a career. I was going to make my own path. So with our wedding date in mind, David and I set out to find our first home.

We called Red Edwards of Cobb County Realty. Red was an icon in the community and a family friend. He was warm and friendly, not just focused on sales; he was like a father figure helping to guide us to the right home.

We told him about our meager budget as college interns, and he said there were no houses for that price, but he'd keep looking for us anyway. We were trying to stay under $25,000, which was low for anything, even in the early 80s.

Eventually we got a call that Red had found two houses in our price range. We made an offer on the first one, but didn't get it. With the second house, a HUD foreclosure, David and I were second in line with our offer. The first buyers ended up not qualifying for their loan, so we got it for $26,150 in 1982. We were one year into college, and didn't qualify for the loan on our own – my grandparents co-signed for us.

We were both 19 years old, with six weeks to go before our wedding date. Since we closed on the house before we got married, my parents reminded us of their expectations for modesty.

"Now, you can't move in until you're married." They told us emphatically. "You absolutely cannot move in until you're married."

We had to purchase our home before the wedding to get it ready to move into. There was a long list of repairs we'd need to make: the whole house needed to be repainted, we had to replace all the plumbing, and we had to install a new furnace. Before we purchased the house, the city of Marietta had condemned it and said it wasn't habitable because it was in such bad shape. The city had taken away the certificate of occupancy, so we couldn't have moved in even if we wanted to. We would have to do a lot of work and have the city come inspect it to say it was safe to live in again – all before our wedding in six weeks.

Thanks to my cousins who flew in from California, and our two families pitching in to help, we managed to finish just in time. We replaced rotten wood, sanded the floors down to the original hardwood, installed a new floor furnace, ran new plumbing, and rewired the entire house. It was a mountain of work, but I loved watching the old building become our first home. We got the house fixed up and had a certificate of occupancy reissued by the city, all in time for our wedding.

David and I were broke, but we were determined to make that house our own. We did everything the cheapest way we could. We saved up for two years to buy a $139 metal storage building for the backyard, since we had no basement, garage, or attic for storage. We even assembled it ourselves from a Sears kit. Our first washer and dryer came used, and were avocado green – so retro!

Now that I was in school and married, it was time to decide what kind of career I would pursue. I took a career test offered by Kennesaw State University, which was then Kennesaw College, and ended up declaring business as my major. At that point, I assumed I would probably end up working for someone else in an office somewhere, because that's what I thought people with business degrees did.

Nearing the halfway mark of my time in college, I decided I needed to narrow down my educational interests to plan for a career. It was about that same time I was taking a course in professional sales. The whole premise of the class was there's no such thing as selling somebody something they don't want to buy. The purpose of professional selling isn't to sell, it's to figure out what somebody needs and then provide a solution. Before that class, I thought sales was about convincing people to buy something, whether they needed it or not. I loved this new idea of approaching sales as a way to help people.

Around the same time my passion for professional sales began to grow, another one of my college professors suggested to the students that we could be "job makers, instead of job takers."

You know how people describe having a moment of clarity, or epiphany? Hearing my professor say that I could be a job maker and not just a job taker was one of those moments for me. Never before had it occurred to me that I could be an entrepreneur.

I started tossing around the idea of getting my real estate license, because I loved the experience of buying my first house and fixing it up. I wanted to help people find their home. And I wanted a college degree to open more doors than my parents had available to them.

During my senior year, I went ahead and earned my real estate license so I'd be ready to start working immediately after graduation. I graduated with my business degree in June of 1985, got my Georgia real estate license the same month, and was immediately hired to work at Northside Realty, under broker and now U.S. Senator Johnny Isakson.

When I was hired by Northside Realty, I'd only had my real estate license for a few weeks. Having owned my own house for three years already, at the age of 22, gave me credibility to get the job; it helped get my foot in the door. I had my first closing about four months later. Helping a family find their dream home brought me so much joy.

David took a great job with International Business Machines Corporation (IBM) straight out of college. We both loved our work.

Sixteen months later, our first son, Jonathan, was born in October 1986. Just 18 months after that, our second son, Matthew, was born in April 1988. David and I were growing our family and our careers. With young children, I opted to work part-time during the day, and instead work more on nights and weekends, so the children always had a parent home.

I made the million dollar club my first full year in real estate – the same year I became a mother. People think being in the club means you earned a million, but it just means you sold a million dollars worth of property. It could mean 10 houses worth $100,000 each, or 20 houses worth $50,000 each. Either way, it was a huge achievement for a young real estate agent to make the million dollar club in her first year, and every year after that.

My success surprised some people, since having young children and working hard enough to make the million dollar club seemed like an impossible load for one person. But David and I shared parenting responsibilities, allowing both our family and our careers to thrive. Not only was I able to succeed in real estate while raising children, but having a young family actually helped me find my first niche in real estate.

As a new mother, I had joined La Leche League – a support group for nursing moms. Whenever families from the group needed a real estate agent, they came to me for help. To those clients, I became known as the "La Leche League Realtor," and I was able to help many families find their perfect home. Instead of parenthood being an obstacle in my career path, I found a way to combine my two passions to benefit both.

To be great at what you do, you don't need to be the best, you just need to love what you do and learn how to balance it with your personal life.

Takeaways:
- Professional sales is about recognizing a need and providing a solution
- Find your passion, set goals, and follow through
- You don't have to work 9 to 5 to be successful

3 HOME IS WHERE COMMUNITY IS

When Jonathan and Matthew were 2 and 3 years old, I helped organize a home preschool with four other moms and six children total. We registered with the state as a private home preschool, and even made matching T-shirts for everyone.

We called ourselves "Around the World Preschool," and each mom was responsible for teaching a different lesson. The preschool location would rotate homes each week, so we created learning centers in big plastic storage bins that were easy to transport.

Each mom had her specialty; one would teach music, another science, and I taught about building, constructing, or creating, because our family had lots of great building toys like K'Nex, Legos, and Lincoln Logs. We took the job as our children's first teachers seriously, and would pre-organize a full year of learning themes including field trips to museums, science centers, and the zoo.

Whoever hosted preschool at their home would be the designated lead teacher that week, with another parent acting as an assistant teacher. The next week, the assistant became the lead teacher, and another mom cycled in as the new assistant. This pattern continued all year, that way the children would see a familiar face each week.

We would do the learning centers for about three hours, then the host mom would make lunch, and sometimes the children would help. They might be given cheese slices and cookie cutters, and we would turn it into a lesson about shapes, or we might make ants on a log using celery, peanut butter, and raisins. Everything we did was intentional and meant to teach our children important lessons.

We all lived in the same neighborhood and had a tight-knit community. The parents and children all got along, and at its core, the home preschool focused on collaboration and cooperation. It was one of the most meaningful things I did as a young parent.

Being involved in my children's early education, and working together with other parents in the community, made us feel like we had created the perfect home for our family.

To our surprise, in 1990 we learned that David's department was closing at IBM. He was given the option to join another department, but told he would have to relocate to remain employed. People were being laid off all around him, and we feared he could be next. With a young family, his steady income was a necessity. There was no question of what we would do – so we prepared to uproot our family and move to a new state.

Relocating to North Carolina from Georgia was a jarring change. We left our friends, our extended families, and the home preschool we worked so hard to create. We went from having a community that felt like family, to knowing nobody. Not to mention our third child, Michelle, was four months away from her due date when we packed the moving truck and headed north. Our home and our family were changing at the same time.

Real estate was more expensive in North Carolina, so despite having two young children and a growing need for space, we had no choice but to downsize from our already modest Georgia home to make ends meet. We settled for a starter home in Cary, North Carolina, where we would stay for two years before moving locally to a larger home.

With all the commotion that came along with moving to North Carolina and giving birth to Michelle a few months later, I let my Georgia real estate license become inactive. With three children ages 4 and under, it would've been too much to keep up with a real estate career. And, since I didn't know the area yet anyway, it seemed like a good idea to spend some time at home raising the children and putting down roots in the community.

But the neighborhood we moved into was already established, and none of our neighbors seemed to have an interest in getting to know us.

At the local playground, other moms would talk to each other as their children played together, while I stood alone watching my children play by themselves. I went to the local grocery store, and I was surrounded by strangers. At my children's school, I didn't know anyone. Everywhere I went, I felt like I was in a foreign country.

In Georgia, every grocery trip included several hellos to friends and neighbors. A morning at the playground was accompanied by friendly conversation between parents. We knew everyone at our children's school. I was so used to the community I had in Georgia, the loss of those daily connections hit me hard. I was lonely in North Carolina, with no sense of belonging.

Living in a smaller home wasn't easy either. It was a three bedroom, two bathroom home, with no basement, no garage, and no attic. We were a bustling family of five, plus the dog. After a couple years in North Carolina, living in an already-established neighborhood where nobody was interested in connecting with the new family on the block, we realized we wouldn't be happy unless we could build our own community again.

David and I found a more spacious home in a new home neighborhood, and we were determined to make it work. Our oldest, Jonathan, was in kindergarten now, and for the first time since relocating, our family began growing roots. David and I participated in Jonathan's school, going in to volunteer every other week or so. We made friends in our neighborhood and at Jonathan's school, and the children loved the wooded area where we lived.

A few years passed, and with all three children in school I decided to get my real estate license in North Carolina. Having moved to Cary ourselves, I saw how it was a popular area for relocation, being located near Research Triangle Park – a hub for high-tech research and development that has been home to more than 200 companies, including IBM. I saw people moving in all around me.

I had learned something about being relocated and that made me want to help others. It's complicated to do, much more than just moving across town. You lose nearby loved ones, but you also have to change your driver's license, your insurance, your doctors, your dentist, your schools, your tax returns – everything you do has to change. With my own experience in real estate and relocation, I thought I could help a few people a year who were facing similar circumstances, and at the same time supplement our family income.

Part time was all I intended to do… but for me, part-time rarely ever happens because I tend to go all in when I'm passionate about something. I ended up doing real estate full time for two years with a Better Homes and Gardens franchise brokerage. As soon as I got back into real estate, my business took off. My second year, I joined a new Coldwell Banker franchise and was named No. 1 agent for the local company. I was busy building my business and putting roots down with my family.

As a hub for business, Cary was a place of worldwide diversity. We felt like it was an amazing city to raise children in; the elementary school had more than 100 nationalities represented so our children would learn about cultures from around the world. We loved the area – the mountains, the nearby beach, and the progressive attitudes. We had finally reached a point where North Carolina felt like home.

Takeaways:
- Collaboration beats flying solo
- Finding a home means finding the right community

4 PEOPLE MOVE FOR A REASON

It was 5:30 a.m. on a Saturday morning in 1995, when I woke up panicked to the feeling of blood curdling in my veins. My 6-year-old son Matthew was screaming frantically from his bedroom down the hall.

Seconds before, I had been sound asleep next to my husband David. Our bodies reacted to the screams more quickly than our minds could process what was happening, as we rushed to Matthew's room. His 55-pound body was stiff and curled like a tiny contortionist. He was hysterical, crying and yelling. He couldn't move his left side.

We reassured him it would be OK. After all, his limbs were probably just numb from him sleeping on his side in a way that temporarily cut off the circulation.

"You probably slept on it funny," we reassured him.

After a few minutes, he was able to move his whole body again. We all went back to sleep and thought nothing more of the strange morning.

The day that followed was typical; Matthew's Cub Scout Troop held a Pinewood Derby race. His homemade wooden race car performed well, but Matthew seemed a bit tired, probably just because he had woken up in the middle of the night.

We kept an eye on him that evening; Matthew's leg went numb and tingly again as he watched TV on the couch. I decided to take him to the doctor first thing Monday morning.

Still believing Matthew had just slept on his side wrong, I took him to the doctor alone, expecting an uneventful visit. After a regular pediatric exam the doctor ordered a brain MRI, which we did right after the doctor visit. Matthew and I returned home after the brain scan.

Before our older son Jonathan even got off the bus from school that afternoon, the phone rang.

"Hello?"
"I need you to sit down," the doctor's voice on the other end said.
"Are you serious?"
"I'm serious."

I sat down at the kitchen table. "Ok."
"Are you sitting down?"
"Yes."

"Matthew has a brain tumor."

Matthew has a brain tumor. *Matthew has a brain tumor. Matthew has a brain tumor.*

I was told to bring him in immediately for a second MRI, and this time the doctors would use contrast to see how bad the tumor was in his brain. Four hours later, David and I waited as our 6-year-old was sedated so he would be perfectly still as they scanned his brain inside a machine 20 times his size.

When it was finished, we went home helpless, waiting for a phone call with the results.

When the home phone finally rang, I couldn't manage to answer. My stomach had been in knots all day and I was sick with fear. David picked up the phone for the both of us. It wasn't good news, and the doctor referred us to a pediatric neurosurgeon.

On that day, I went from a real estate agent and parent, to being a medical advocate and internet researcher as my child battled a brain tumor with an 85 percent survival rate. That may sound like a high survival rate, but as a mother, all I heard was a 15 percent chance my child would not live to be 7 years old.

I scoured the primitive internet, before easy-to-use search engines like Google existed, to find medical journal articles and information from brain tumor association websites. It was a time consuming, tedious, and complicated task, but my need to be an informed advocate for my child pushed me to learn the most modern internet search techniques.

I printed and read everything I could find, and went to each doctor appointment with detailed medical questions for Matthew's doctors and surgeons. I wanted to know every detail about his diagnosis and treatment. My child's brain tumor was out of my control, but I could make sure he got the best treatment possible.

Just 15 days after that first doctor visit, Matthew was having his skull opened and a tumor cut out of his growing brain, at the University of North Carolina Chapel Hill Hospital. The smell of sterile latex gloves, hospital soap, and medical supplies, came together to create a plastic-like perfume so pungent it made me sick.

Georgia family members poured into Cary, North Carolina to help. They watched our two other children, Michelle, 4, and Jonathan, 8, as my husband and I took care of Matthew during and after his surgery. I remember my older brother Steve filled our refrigerator and freezer with meals so we wouldn't have to worry about food for a while.

Matthew made it through the six-hour surgery; they got the entire tumor out, and three weeks after the surgery he was back in school.

Every two months, we took Matthew for follow-up MRI brain scans to watch for recurrence of his tumor. Months went by and his scans came back clear. It seemed we had been dealt an impossible hand, and we won.

Nine months after his surgery Matthew started to mention slight numbness and tingling in his leg. Worried the tumor was back, I insisted the doctors take a closer look. But with no visual signs of another tumor on Matthew's scans, the doctors concluded it must be scar tissue in his brain causing the symptoms.

The numbness gradually got worse month by month. There was no sign of another tumor on Matthew's scans; but, David and I had our suspicions. We were so sure we'd get bad news, that David had been coming with me to every one of Matthew's scans.

Eighteen months went by after his surgery with no sign of another tumor, but for the last nine months David and I anticipated the worst. In August,

Matthew's scan was clear, and in September, his tumor was back and it was twice the size. This time, the doctors said it was likely a much more aggressive type of tumor.

Matthew was 8 years old now. David and I sat him down and explained that he had another brain tumor.

"Sometimes tumors come back and you have to go to the hospital for another surgery. Do you understand?"

"God gave me this brain tumor so another kid wouldn't get one," Matthew told us. "He gave it to me because he knows I can handle it."

The surgery to remove the tumor carried with it a 50 percent likelihood of long-term brain damage and permanent disabilities; the risk of a stroke or paralysis was great.

When I asked the doctor about the survival rate for a second brain tumor surgery, he said it was better if I didn't know and suggested I try to focus only on my own child's survival. Doctors warned that left-side paralysis was a likely outcome. My child could be paralyzed on his left side, because the surgeon would need to carve into healthy brain tissue to be sure he removed the entire tumor, to increase Matthew's chance of survival.

The first tumor felt like an obstacle we had conquered; but the second tumor felt like a lifelong battle just beginning. It was a difficult time to live so far from our parents and extended family.

After the invasive six hour surgery, Matthew woke up and couldn't move his left side. His doctors said the trauma it caused on his brain could result in temporary, or permanent, paralysis. So for days, we waited, worried, and prayed.

On the fourth day after the surgery, Matthew started to feel his left fingers and toes for the first time. By the end of the day, he was up walking around the hospital room. He came out of it without any major complications, other than minor weakness on his left side.

He had beaten the odds, again. Despite this victory, David and I were acutely aware of how fragile Matthew's life was; the chance of brain tumor recurrence in children who have had more than one tumor is common. So, we braced ourselves for the possibility that Matthew may be battling brain tumors for the rest of his life.

Our family's future uncertain, David and I vowed to move back to Georgia to be near family. I decided to give up my real estate career in North Carolina in 1996. We needed to go back home.

Takeaways:
- Life can change in an instant
- Knowledge empowers
- People move for a reason

5 LIFE TRANSITIONS

People don't ever just move for fun; moving is always related to a major life transition. Someone may buy or sell a house because of a marriage or partnership, or because of a separation; they may need more space after a birth or adoption, or need to downsize after a death or loss of a job; they could be looking for their dream house after a job promotion, or trying to find the right community after a transfer or because of a health situation. Whatever the reason, there's always a deeper story attached to why someone wants to buy or sell their home.

IBM, where David had worked for more than a decade, supported our move back to Georgia to be near family. Not only did they agree to let David move and work from home, they also provided us with moving expenses. But just because we needed and wanted to move back to Georgia, didn't mean it was easy.

I had become a successful real estate agent in North Carolina, but since I didn't have an active real estate license in Georgia I had to rely on somebody else to buy a house.

In 1997, David and I went to see a local agent in Georgia. We explained that we were relocating back to Georgia from North Carolina, and had previously lived in Cobb County. We asked to see what she had on the market in Cherokee County that wasn't stucco, because we weren't interested in homes with stucco.

At the time, synthetic stucco siding was known for retaining too much moisture and potentially causing structural issues for homeowners. So, whether the stucco was real or synthetic, homes with that type of siding were much more difficult to resell. As a real estate agent myself, I was all too familiar with this issue; David and I weren't interested in any homes with stucco facades. We didn't want to have a problem selling our home in the future.

When I told the Georgia real estate agent we didn't want stucco, she asked why.

"Because even if it's real stucco, there's a perception that it has more problems, like synthetic stucco, and I don't want to buy something that has a perception issue."

"Let me tell you something," she said. "I am the top agent in this area, and I have been for a long time. I don't know how much experience you have, but it's probably not as much as mine. All you have to do is educate people, starting with yourself, and then educate your clients. It's not a problem."

"Well, perception is a problem. It's always a problem. And I can manage the problem by not buying a stucco house."

My request was reasonable, and the conversation should've stopped there.

But that agent kept arguing with me, and I got fed up. We walked out and decided she wasn't a good fit for helping us find a home.

When we got back in the car, I said to David: "I'm not going to be back in real estate for a while, but when I am, I'm going to take her spot as the top agent."

That's exactly what I did.

It would be six years before I started practicing real estate again in Georgia, but when I did, I took that agent's place as the No. 1 agent in the local real estate association.

Moving back to Georgia from the higher-priced market in North Carolina meant we could afford more space. We chose to buy a new home in the Bradshaw Farm subdivision in Hickory Flat – a small town with great schools and lots of nature nearby. My brother Steve and his family lived just down the street so we were close to family, and the community was in a central location between my parents who lived about

30 minutes north, and David's parents who lived 30 minutes south. It was the perfect location for us; we were surrounded by family.

Our children were all outdoor, nature-loving children, and we needed a home with trees and bugs and animals. They needed a place to build tree forts and dig in the dirt. At first, we didn't think we would find a home in Bradshaw Farm because it had been a farm, with mostly cleared pasture land – very few lots had the tree coverage we were looking for – but when a wooded lot finally came on the market, we scooped it up as quickly as we could.

The backyard was covered in trees and underbrush. Beneath the canopy of old hardwood trees grew wild privet bushes and young pine saplings. The yard was full of life: an endless supply of bugs, the occasional nonvenomous garden snake, and even a nest of bunnies had made it their home.

After moving in, one afternoon we looked out back and saw our three children had climbed under the privet bushes and carved out a fort. The joy in our children's eyes affirmed our decision to buy that house in Bradshaw Farm.

What further solidified our choice to move to that small but growing north metro community was a visit to Hickory Flat Elementary School.

At the time, Matthew had to be on anti-seizure medication after his second major brain surgery. The medicine made him unable to stay awake for a full school day. As a parent, I was worried about Matthew being back in school.

In an extraordinary coincidence, the principal said she also had a child who had gone through brain surgery, so she understood the significance and special concerns. My eyes welled up with gratitude. This principal, and school, and house, were put in our path for a reason. I knew this was home.

We weren't sure how many more brain surgeries Matthew would need, or what the future held, but our family had found our home. I committed to taking at least five years off work to focus on raising my family and to be available for whatever came next with Matthew.

Although it would be several years before I went back into real estate, finding that community in Hickory Flat taught me the most important lesson of my entire career: as real estate agents, we shouldn't start by asking clients how big of a house someone wants or how many bathrooms they need, we should ask what kind of community they're looking for, how they want to live, and what life transitions they're going through.

If you can't build community where you live, it will never be home. We're in the business of helping people find their home, their community… not just a house with the right number of bedrooms and bathrooms.

Understanding why someone is moving allows agents to provide better service to their clients. Just like I learned in my professional sales class in college, you have to understand a client's needs in order to provide the right solution.

Takeaways:
- Real Estate is about life transitions, not just transactions
- People cross our path for a reason

6 SOMETIMES A PATH CHOOSES YOU

After settling into our home in Georgia, I wanted to immediately get involved in the community and my children's school. Having felt alienated before, when we first moved to North Carolina, I was determined to build connections as soon as possible in our new location.

I joined the Parent-Teacher Association and was put on the executive board; became a Girl Scout leader; coached basketball and other sports for my children; and volunteered at the school whenever I could.

Five months after moving into our new house, news spread about one of our school board members violating school district policy by acting outside the chain of command. There were reports he had taken home a school district employee's tax documents with no explanation, tried to discipline children by pulling over a school bus himself, and demanded school employees be fired for playing music he didn't approve of during a basketball game. When word got out about the board member's behavior, parents and teachers were furious.

An anonymous complaint to the Southern Association for Colleges and Schools resulted in the entire school district being put on academic probation. That meant our schools were at risk for losing accreditation, which could impact a high school graduate's ability to get hired or accepted into the college of their choice. Losing accreditation was serious.

We had just moved back to Georgia, bought a house, and were trying to get some stability back for Matthew and our family... and now, the school system was on probation. Once again, it felt like our children's futures were being threatened.

I was already all in, but when news of the probation got out, I felt it was my responsibility to get even more involved to make sure my children's school would remain accredited.

I joined up with a local movement that started with the goal to recall the problematic school board member. At the time, the school district had four high schools, and I took on the responsibility of collecting thousands of signatures for the recall effort in one of the four high school areas.

Georgia law allowed for a 45-day window to collect about 18,000 signatures from registered voters in the district, which would result in a recall vote to give voters the chance to oust the school board member and get our district back on the right path.

This would be no easy task, and ensuring success meant clever planning. We decided to start our 45-day window just before Thanksgiving, knowing that retail stores would be bustling with people doing holiday shopping before Christmas, so that's what we did.

Sure enough, it worked. We delivered more than 21,000 signatures to the Cherokee County elections office at the end of the 45-day period, and line by line, they verified each signature as being a valid registered voter. We had won our right to a recall election.

Before the scheduled recall election, the board member ended up resigning and a special election to fill his seat was announced.

When the special election was announced, I had just met the one year residency requirement for school board members. Everyone I had met through the PTA and recall effort told me I had to run.

In North Carolina, I had served on the school board advisory council for Wake County, which was triple the size of Cherokee County, so I had some strong experience working with school systems.

I wasn't much for politics, but I loved our community in Georgia, so I agreed to run for the vacant school board seat. I wanted to do my part to improve the community my family was a part of, and if that meant getting into politics, that's what I'd do.

I found myself in a three-way race against two retired educators, both of whom were gentlemen, and a pleasure to run against. On March 16, 1999, I was elected with 63 percent of the vote to fill the vacant seat on the Cherokee County school board.

Through teamwork and collaboration, the school board corrected its governance problems. After a re-evaluation by the Southern Association for Colleges and Schools, our district was removed from probation and went on to have four years of consecutive progress. Across the entire district, schools earned higher national test scores, improved graduation rates, and made student success even more of a priority. The school district became recognized as one of the top school systems in the country, and I finally felt like my children's futures were safe.

I loved my experience in public service. So, when a seat in the local Georgia House of Representatives came open in 2002, I decided to run for the seat.

Once again, I found myself in a three-way race. In the primary election I came out with the most votes among the three candidates, with 42 percent. However, in order to win in a primary, I would've needed more than 50 percent of the votes. So, a runoff election was set to be held three weeks later between myself and the candidate who had come in second-place in the primary.

My campaign manager said that 85 percent of the time, when you win in a primary, you'll lose the election, so we needed to be all-in during the weeks leading up to the runoff.

Just two days after the primary election, I was in a meeting with my campaign manager. We were strategizing our plan leading up to the runoff election when my phone rang.

It was my mom on caller ID. She knew I was in a meeting with my campaign manager, but I decided to pick up the phone anyway.

"Hey, Mom."

For a few seconds, she said nothing.

Then, in a shaky, faint voice, she spoke. "Steve died."

My parents were in their 60s at the time, so I figured it must be a friend of theirs named Steve.

"Steve who?"

Even through the phone, I felt the knot building in the back of my mom's throat as she tried to tell me. "Your brother, Steve."

My brother? No.
"That can't be true, are you sure?"

"I'm sure."

My stomach turned like I was free-falling with no parachute.
"No." I paused. "That can't be true."
She wept in pain, "I'm sure." She handed the phone to my dad.

"I don't know what we're going to do. We can't live through this," he said, his voice shaking.

By that point, I was sobbing. My campaign manager knew something was very wrong. He offered to drive me to my parent's house, but I insisted on having my car.

I barely remember driving. I called David from the car, and told him I had to stay with my parents overnight. For all I know, I was going 100 miles per hour on the interstate, I don't remember; it's a miracle I made it safely to my parent's house. By the time I got there, more than a dozen friends had already arrived.

The first person to get there was the pastor from the community chapel.

"Nobody knows how you feel except for God, because He lost His son, too." The pastor lost his son several years earlier, and knew how to comfort my parents better than anyone else.

Of all the condolences from friends, that meant more than anything else to my parents after Steve died.

From all those people who showed up for my parents and my family, I learned something about grief that I didn't know before: the importance of being present.

So many people, some of my parent's dearest friends, didn't show up, didn't call. Some mailed a sympathy card, "our greatest sympathy, thinking of you." Some said they couldn't be there because they "don't do funerals." And worst of all, some said, "God doesn't give you more than you can handle." But, this *was* more than we could handle.

We do a sorry job of teaching people how to handle grief. I didn't even know how to talk to my own children about it at the time.

The loss of my brother sent me and our entire family into shock. It was the biggest tailspin I'd been in my whole life. Matthew's brain tumors were terrifying, but he lived. My brother Steve had died, from a heart attack in his 40s, with no warning.

My parents weren't able to handle the funeral planning, so I had to take over responsibility for the details. Steve died in North Dakota, and I had to make arrangements to ship his body to Georgia, then get it to the funeral home. I had to make decisions about where to embalm him; I had to decide whether it would be an open or closed casket; I had to plan the funeral, pick the pastor, make a brochure… it's like planning an entire wedding in a 24-hour period, but instead of a joyful event, it's excruciating.

Shock, anger, and denial are the first symptoms of grief, and they happen fast. Within a couple of days, our family was feeling the effects of these stages, and we agreed an open casket was needed for some sort of closure. We chose a close friend and retired nun to host the service, and we picked meaningful music Steve liked – rock, soul, and country.

I remember walking into the side room at Darby Funeral Home in Canton for the family viewing. We were probably 15 feet away when my mom saw Steve's face start to show over the edge of the casket. She screamed like I've never heard another human being do before or since. It was the most stomach-churning, sound-shattering wail I have ever heard. In that shriek, I could feel the pain of my mother's broken heart.

She could barely stand as she looked at his body. My dad appeared stoic, but he's a sensitive man and I could tell as his eyes welled with tears, that his heart was filled with grief.

At the end of the service, we left time for anyone who wanted to speak, and many did. People took turns telling stories and talking about Steve, and when everyone else had finished, my mom stood up.

I was afraid she would collapse if she tried to speak, but she insisted.

"The depth of our grief is a mirror of the depth of our love. We wouldn't feel the gut-wrenching, life-changing pain if we didn't love Steve. And that's the only thing that can get me through this right now:

knowing the excruciating pain I feel is a reflection of the love I have for Steve."

After more than a decade, my mom's words still ring in my mind when I think of my brother, or when I'm trying to comfort someone who's recently lost a loved one. The words we say to people when a loved one dies burn into their mind.

Just 18 days after my brother died, the runoff election was held. Those weeks leading up to the election were a complete blur. I couldn't bring myself to work on the campaign at all.

When the results came in, I had lost by five votes. An automatic recount is available per state law when the results are that close. After the recount concluded, I got a call from the elections office.

"We did find the count was correct, but five people crossed over from the Democratic primary to the Republican runoff."

This meant I could challenge the election and have it thrown out, and a new election could be held.

I knew many of my supporters didn't vote in the runoff, thinking I had already won the election after doing so well in the primary, and with the report of voter crossover from the elections office, I had a good chance of winning if I called for a new election.

Sometimes in life, our path is obvious. Other times, we come to a crossroads and the right choice is unclear.

I had been on track for a successful real estate career when my son was diagnosed with his brain tumor and my path changed. Then, I was on the path for public service, but my world turned upside down when my brother died. I had prayed for God's will in the election, and I felt like this was a sign telling me to change direction again.

God laid out this path for me. Losing by five votes, when there were exactly five illegally cast votes that could've flipped the election, felt like God saying "you could've won, but it's not where you're needed." I needed to be with my family, so I declined a new election.

Takeaways:
- The right path isn't always what you planned
- No one is guaranteed a long time on earth
- Be present for those who are grieving

SHARING MY PATH

7 FIND COLLEAGUES WHO SHARE YOUR VALUES

My son survived two brain tumors but there was still a chance he would have a recurring tumor; my brother had died; I gave up my seat on the school board and lost the race for a seat in the Georgia House of Representatives.

I saw my parents every day, and the weight of their sorrow was crushing.

Someone needed to make sure Steve's belongings were taken care of, and that my parents were being taken care of after this loss. My response was to go into "take-charge" mode because someone needed to. I didn't allow myself to grieve. Just when most of my family had passed the first few stages of grief, it all finally hit me.

I was overcome with anxiety every time the phone rang, wondering if someone else had died. I worried about who would die next because if my brother died at 44, other people could die at any age. Of course, I always knew that people could die at any age, but when I experienced it personally, it became different, more real.

The fear of another loved one dying felt all-encompassing. I worried when my family was driving, or when someone didn't answer the phone. I worried Matthew's brain tumors would come back – it had only been five years since his last one.

My husband knew I needed something to focus on besides worrying about everyone. He knew how passionate I had been about real estate, and suggested I get back into it. Steve died in August 2002, and by March 2003, I had reinstated my Georgia real estate license and began the search for a brokerage.

During my time in public service, I had met a local real estate brokerage owner, David Moody. Throughout my campaign for the Georgia House of Representatives, Moody had supported me. He wrote me a check for $250, and without knowing me, gave me a copy of his office keys and said I was welcome to use his office for phone calls or making copies.

That act of kindness created a trust between us, which is a rare thing in politics. His kindness represented something deeper about him as a person, and that stuck with me.

So, after my husband suggested I get back into real estate, I spoke with David Moody about it. I chose to sit in on sales meetings at several different brokerages to see which one would be the best fit: I was looking for the right workplace culture. I wanted to work with people who cared about each other, about their clients, and about improving their skills.

Sitting in on the sales meeting at Moody's brokerage, ERA Sunrise Realty, made me sure it was the perfect fit. I joined the brokerage, and focused my energy on building my business.

Moody and his brokerage fostered collaboration and support, and it felt like a family, not just a fabricated slogan like other companies I'd seen. During my first nine months back in real estate after a six-year hiatus, I closed 37 sales.

The workload was ramping up so quickly, I found myself overwhelmed. Moody said I needed a buyer agent, like an assistant, and suggested I team up with another agent at ERA Sunrise Realty, Lisa Millsap.

I had been out of the business so long I had never heard of having someone work for you in real estate – unless you were a broker.

Lisa and I set up a meeting, and I could tell immediately she was the perfect fit. Like me, she believed in ethical business and treating people with respect – we felt instantly aligned. Lisa and I teamed up in October to become The Becky Babcock Real Estate Team, and we closed 95 deals in our first year together.

That same year, we added a part-time administrator, and with that, our team model was born. I didn't want to compete against my own team member, so we agreed that I would handle all the sellers as a seller specialist, and Lisa would work with all the buyers as a buyer specialist. It was a perfect solution. For the first time in months, I felt like I had a focus and purpose again.

It had been a little over a year after Steve's death, and I was talking to my mom.

"Your dad is just lost. He can't find his way. It's like he's lost the wind in his sails. He doesn't have meaning in life; I'm really worried about him. I think he's actually depressed and he needs something to redirect, something to focus on."

"Why doesn't he get his real estate license and work for me?"

Focusing on real estate had helped me refocus my life after Steve's death, so why wouldn't it do the same for my dad?

He agreed to study and learn about real estate, and at age 70, my dad passed the real estate exam.

During the next two years, our team added a second administrative position and four more agents, including my dad. Several years later, my mom joined him in real estate, and they worked together on my team. Real estate helped give my family an avenue for moving forward after that devastating loss.

After our first full year as a team, in 2004 we earned ERA's Leader Circle award for being in the top 1 percent for sales in the U.S. for the national ERA franchise. Year after year for the next decade, business increased and the team grew.

Every year we were winning national awards for ERA, but I didn't go to the awards ceremony because I was focused on the work, not the awards. It was a chaotic and busy time.

"It's a pretty big deal. You know, you could go to the international convention and get your awards," Moody told me with not a hint of pushiness.

"Well I estimated the cost for airfare and a hotel, and I could go buy a new computer for that kind of money," I told him.

"That's okay, you don't have to go," he would respond gently.

For years, I passed up the chance to attend the convention and awards ceremony, and while he always asked if I would attend, Moody was supportive when I declined. ERA just kept mailing me the awards.

But when 2006 came to a close, we ranked in ERA's top 10 for sales in the entire country, and took the title of No. 1 real estate agent in Cherokee County for sales – both accomplishments we maintained year after year.

Just as past years, Moody asked if I planned to attend the international ERA convention. This time, nudging me a bit more to go.

"It might be a good idea for you to go to one of the conventions and see the bigger picture, to understand why we're part of the ERA franchise and what it means."

I reluctantly agreed.

When I arrived at the ERA International Business Convention, the welcome I received was overwhelming. They treated me like some rock star real estate agent, all because I sold a bunch of houses and created a team.

The idea of having a real estate team, rather than a single agent, had just started to grow within ERA and everyone was curious about how it worked.

At the convention, I met like-minded people from around the world and we shared ideas for improving our trade. All those years I missed the conference, I had thought it was just about awards. Meeting other people with my level of passion was energizing, and I never missed an ERA convention after that.

Takeaways:
- Workplace culture is more than just a marketing message, it's how you act when nobody else is watching
- Seek colleagues who share your values and vision
- Learning about things you're passionate about is energizing

8 WORK *ON* YOUR BUSINESS, NOT JUST IN IT

From 2003 to 2013, the team got bigger and bigger in order to handle our growing workload. In 2013, 16 years after his second and last brain tumor, my son Matthew got his real estate license and joined the team. We continued to add more team members, and sales continued to increase.

Despite our team's success, I was growing weary. For a decade, it felt like I never had a chance to step off the real estate hamster wheel. I'd been answering phone calls, listing and showing houses, handling paperwork, and building a team nonstop for 10 years, and I was exhausted.

By 2013, I was meeting with more than 150 sellers a year, and personally interacting with every client. The team closed just over 200 transactions that year, and I was working 80-hour weeks.

For years, I was rarely home for dinner. I'd get 20 or 30 calls every Saturday and Sunday. If I stopped to take a break, the backlog of messages was so overwhelming I could barely catch up, so it was easier to never take a break in the first place.

I desperately needed time with my family. Something had to give.

In March of 2013, my team attended the Cherokee Association of Realtors annual awards ceremony, being recognized as the No. 1 residential agent team in Cherokee County for the eighth consecutive year. While I was thrilled to have our team's effort being acknowledged, at the same time, I was on the edge of a major burnout.

After the awards were given out, I ended up talking with another agent. He congratulated me on our award, and asked what was next for us, for "The Becky Babcock Team."

I didn't know it at the time, but looking back now, it was at that exact moment when my path turned again.

I'd been thinking for some time that I might need to hire someone to help me manage the team – something I'd confided in my husband but nobody else… until that agent asked what was next for my team. There must've been some sort of divine intervention that day to make me say it out loud.

"I need to hire a 'big fish' to help me manage the team."

Right then, the idea of hiring someone to help me became real. I felt like I put my post in the ground that day, pointing the way to my future path.

Two months later, a local broker named Brad Nix called.

Brad was a co-founder of an influential real estate technology conference – Real Estate Tech

South, or RETSO. He had been the broker of his own real estate company and he helped brand several successful and modern local companies. He also happened to be a past president of the Cherokee Association of Realtors. Getting a call from Brad was a big deal.

"I heard you're looking to hire someone to help you with your real estate business and I think I might know someone, but I have a few questions first," he said.

I hadn't even put the word out that I was looking for someone. There was no job posting, and the only person I'd told about my future intention to hire someone to help manage my team was that agent at the awards ceremony two months earlier. So for Brad to call me, must have meant he had someone good in mind.

He asked me all kinds of questions: what did I have in mind for the future of my team, what did I need help with, what problems were we dealing with, had I thought about how I wanted to brand my team... he was very thorough.

"Becky, you know how I had told you I had someone in mind for you? I'm actually the one thinking about applying for your open position."

Here's someone who I see as a real estate rock star, and he's asking to work on my team?

At the time, Brad was working as the chief brand strategist for a bank. He was in corporate America, wearing a suit and tie, making good money.

I was a little skeptical. Why would he want to leave a good-paying job to come work with me? He was already on my level; we had been in the real estate business about the same amount of time.

So we met for coffee to talk more about the possibility of working together, and Brad said he missed real estate. He wasn't happy with his corporate life, and he wanted to control his own destiny again.

I told him about how busy I was, and explained what I was looking for: I needed help to position the team brand away from my name and to build processes so we could scale up effectively with our continued growth.

The more Brad and I talked, the more it seemed meant to be for us to work together. Our skills were complementary, and our values and approach to business were aligned. From May until August, we talked about what made my team so unique and successful, and the things we were lacking: a good Customer Relationship Management database (CRM), a system beyond checklists, and a brand that represented the collective team effort.

While my team's system was working, it was slowing us down. We were No. 1 in the local real estate association and ranked in the top 10 for the ERA franchise in the entire U.S. – yet our organizational workflow was seriously lacking.

As the leader of the team, it was my job to plan for our growth, but I was so busy trying to keep up with day-to-day showings, client emails, calls, and listings, that I wasn't able to take a step back and look at the bigger picture. One of my favorite business books, which helped me realize I needed to look at the bigger picture for my team, was "The E-Myth Revisited," by Michael Gerber. In it, Gerber explains how leaders must work *on* their business, not just *in* their business. What he means is that a business will thrive if its leaders are thinking about the bigger picture, rather than getting caught up in all the daily chaos.

I knew I needed to work *on* the business plan, instead of just working *in* the business doing daily tasks, but I was buried under the sheer volume of transactions. For a decade I'd worked inside my business, building the team, but I knew it was time to think about our future.

Each time we met, Brad diligently took notes as we worked on a detailed plan for moving forward. We laid out a clear path for improvement and on Aug. 7, 2013, Brad was hired as a managing director.

It was time to tell my team.

I never held regular meetings with my team, because we were all too busy. So when I scheduled "a very important team meeting," everyone knew something big was going on.

I was a nervous wreck walking into that meeting to introduce Brad and explain our plan. My insides were shaking, and my palms were sweaty. I was afraid my team would push back. I was bringing an outsider into the tight-knit team we'd built over the last decade.

As the meeting got started, I could tell they were all worried about what was happening. Their fear of the unknown was transparent; I could see it on their faces and feel it in the weight of the silence.

As I told the team about what was happening, their fear of the unknown shifted to concern over their own jobs. What would a rebranding mean, what would the workload be, what would change? But none of us, not even Brad and I, knew what was to come.

Everyone was worried about the idea of me stepping back. For as long as the team had existed, I had been right on the front lines with the rest of the agents. Things were going to change.

We got right to work.

We began analyzing the team processes, starting with me.

"What do you do during the day?" Brad asked. "How many hours are you working per week?"

The truth, which I almost feel bad admitting, is that I was putting in between 80 and 100 hours a week.

"That's not scalable, and that's not long-term doable. You're going to want to quit this business." Brad was good at being honest with me, and it was true.

So task-by-task, we began chipping away at my list of duties. Brad made recommendations for lowering my workload, but the problem was that clients always wanted *me*. It was, after all, The Becky Babcock Team. When someone called our team, they expected to work directly with me. I had created a successful monster and it was eating me alive.

I'd been wanting to take the focus off of myself for some time; I was just one member of a team, and I didn't like how the team was named after me. It originally came about out of necessity. When I brought on my first agent and administrative specialist, it was just the three of us, and we were The Becky Babcock Team. It worked out fine at first.

However, as the team grew, the name got old fast. I didn't like it, but the team name was known all around the community. I couldn't just switch the name of a well-known real estate team without a full-blown rebranding, and I didn't have time to do something like that by myself.

Once Brad joined the team, we could finally make it happen. Rebranding and reorganizing the business was the best path forward.

Takeaways:

- Be open to unexpected paths
- Your business is *not* about you, and never was
- Work *on* your business, not just *in* it

9 EVERY SALE HAS A STORY

I wanted the new brand to reflect the uniqueness of each client's personal journey. As a team, we had always customized our approach for each client based on their individual story, but we had never considered sharing those stories as part of our brand.

Focusing on our customer's life transition, instead of just thinking about the transaction, was one of the things that made us different from other real estate teams.

Every client, every story, every person we encounter, is an opportunity to enrich a life transition. And those stories can stick with you for a lifetime.

One client of mine several years ago was a mother trying to help her only child relocate closer to family before she passed away. Her son was in his early 20s, and had lost his father in an accident many years earlier. The client was fighting ALS, or Lou Gehrig's disease, a degenerative disease that causes someone to lose control of their muscles.

The average life expectancy after diagnosis is usually between 2-4 years, and my client wanted her son to be closer to his aunt, so he wouldn't be alone after she passed away. The transition to life without parents wouldn't be easy, but at least we could help him move closer to his aunt and uncle.

I became very close with the family as I helped sell the mother's house, it was an emotional time for everyone. After the closing I asked if there was anything else I could do for the son besides giving real estate guidance, and he said, "help find me a good Christian woman to marry."

I smiled, thinking at first he was joking, but then realized he was serious.

A few months went by and I thought about his request, but finding the right fit wouldn't be easy. Then it happened – the right woman came to mind. I knew her parents well, and had their approval to make an introduction. After several attempts from me to encourage her to accept his friend request on Facebook, they finally met online. The first date came soon after and, would you believe it, a perfect match was made.

In 2017, they celebrated five years of marriage and their son's third birthday.

I was so blessed to be able to help that young man move closer to family, and to bring those two people together to create a new family. I believe they were all put in my path for a reason. Unexpected outcomes like that are the moments worth capturing, worth remembering, worth cherishing.

Another time I felt like I was put in a client's path for a reason happened when I was driving through the neighborhood where my family lived, Bradshaw Farm. I drove by a house for sale in the subdivision that was listed for sale by the owner, who was a part time real estate agent. I saw his wife at the mailbox and stopped to say hello even though I didn't know them personally.

She seemed stressed, and said her husband was in a horrible car accident the night before. He had been paralyzed from the neck down. I asked what I could do to help.

She confided they were selling the home due to financial struggles and explained she was a school teacher with a modest income. She was afraid that since her husband could no longer work, they would lose the house before it would sell. Knowing I lived and worked in the neighborhood, she encouraged me to bring any buyers I could to show their ranch-style home.

But there was a problem... I didn't have any ranch buyers at the time.

My heart was heavy and I couldn't concentrate on work after hearing about this young woman's husband. So I left the neighborhood to do some errands to try and get my mind off the situation for a while. I stopped by a local store to pick up a shower curtain even though I had never stepped foot in that particular store before. While inside, I happened to cross paths with a friend of mine from church.

We chatted a bit, then the woman from church said she always wanted a ranch in Bradshaw Farm. I was stunned, and she could see I was taken aback. I told her what had just happened with my conversation with the neighborhood family, and she agreed to go see the house. She loved it. We brought her husband back later and he liked it, too.

However, the couple from church was worried about buying a house before selling their current one. They felt it was too risky and their current house wasn't even on the market.

Confident that I could sell their house, I encouraged them to seriously consider moving ahead with buying before selling their current house. I asked them to consider the unique circumstances of the young couple selling. After a night of prayerful consideration, they decided to move forward.

I went to present my buyer's offer to the homeowner. We sat on her sofa as she cried and recalled the nightmare she was living. She worried about what life would be like since her husband was paralyzed, whether they could ever have children or if they could survive financially. She signed the contract and we both felt confident we were on the right path.

The couple from church immediately listed their current house with me. Within 24 hours of going on the market, the house sold to another one of my buyers. It was the highest price ever for a resale home in their neighborhood. At that point, everyone knew this was meant to be.

As we approached the closing day, I got a call from the attorney... we had a problem, a big one. He said the sellers owed more for their home than what they were selling it for. They were upside down by $26,600 and needed that much money to pay off their debt at closing. I couldn't believe what was happening to this young couple.

I met with the wife and she was devastated. I calculated my broker's side of the commission at $9,600 for the $320,000 sale, and offered to do the sale at zero percent to save her $9,600, but that still left us $17,000 short. She contacted her church for help and they paid the other $17,000 so she could sell the house. The joy I felt at hearing the news was indescribable.

When someone buys or sells a home, they're going through a huge life transition, and as a real estate agent, we have an important role in dictating how smoothly that transition goes for them. The more we can connect with and understand our clients, the better we can meet their needs for buying or selling a home.

Everyone has a story, and if we as real estate agents choose to listen carefully, we can change lives.

By showing people respect, being united in the same goal, and always trying to live by the golden rule, real estate agents can make a significant impact in their communities.

Takeaways:
- Every sale begins with a story
- Be open to meaningful, unexpected, and sometimes life changing paths
- Ask questions, listen, and truly empathize with your clients

10 WHAT'S IN A BRAND

Before we could get down to the business of building our brand identity, we needed to address my schedule. I would never have time to work on rebranding if I spent all of my time with clients.

By the time Brad came on board, I was doing around 170 transactions a year and going to every listing.

My cell phone number was the only business number out there for our team at the time, so my phone never stopped ringing… I couldn't even take an hour-long walk with my husband without being inundated with calls.

I had evening appointments five out of seven days a week. When my husband asked if I'd be home for dinner, 90 percent of the time my answer had to be no.

To have family time, it had to be a scheduled appointment. Clients wouldn't respect family time as a reason for being unavailable in the evenings or weeknights, so I just got in the habit of saying I had an appointment when I wanted to spend a couple hours with my husband and children.

Both my family and Brad saw the toll those 80-hour work weeks were taking on me: I was close to giving up real estate all together.

One of the first changes was for me to find a more efficient way to hand off clients to our agent specialists.

We decided to handle it like triage during a crisis, where the leader decides which injuries are the most critical and assigns certain duties to each surgeon and doctor. Our first goal was to decide what everyone would do, and what the best course of action would be.

My buyer and seller specialists were the doctors, who worked with clients and listings to make sure everything was handled with care and expertise. My administrative team members were nurses in the emergency room: they problem-solved and kept everyone organized so nothing important would be overlooked. Brad and I were there as consultants and surgeons, there to answer questions and operate on the business model.

As the rebranding process began, Brad interviewed each administrative, buyer, and seller specialist, because we wanted to encompass the entire team in the new brand.

Our goal was to take away my name and make it into a team brand, and we wanted it to be authentic – to represent all of us – we wanted it to be real.

I was still working my usual 80 hours a week, plus meeting with Brad to work on the business for another 10-20 hours a week. It was during that time, over a span of about 90 days, that the new brand emerged. I began handing off a few appointments each week to other team members, and forwarded my phone some days to make time for the rebranding process.

We did exercises to pinpoint what mattered to me and my team… things like family and financial security. For one exercise, I had to think about historical figures that had meaning to me; I picked Mother Teresa and Margaret Thatcher, two women who forged their own paths: one through confidence and the other through love.
I was told to pick which superhero I would be, and I chose Wonder Woman. Brad asked what books I read lately that meant something to me, which movies I liked, what TV shows I watched. We did all these interviews to try and get a sense of what type of leader I was and wanted to be, and what sort of brand already existed but needed to be uncovered and shared.

One of many breakthroughs during this process came from an exercise where I wrote words on a whiteboard. I chose words to describe what kind of business I ran, what was important to me, and how the team delivered services to customers.

The goal was to completely fill a whiteboard with important values and descriptive words. It took hours and felt like I wrote 500 words by the time I finished.

The board was covered in meaningful words and phrases: respect, love, family, integrity, strength, excellence, attentiveness, direction, help, guiding clients, unity, work-life balance, effort, conscientious, the golden rule, awareness, growth-oriented, open minded, constant improvement, teamwork, looking out for one another, cutting edge, technology, communicative... the list went on and on.

Brad had me stand next to the whiteboard, and asked me to erase half of the words I had just worked so hard to come up with, the ones that weren't as meaningful to me.

Finished with that task, I stepped back to admire my list of words, when he asked me to erase half, again. Over and over, Brad challenged me to erase half of the dwindling set of words until there were only 10 left.

"Now, out of these 10, pick just three that you think represent your values in life and your values for leading the team," Brad said. "If your life values and business values aren't aligned, then they aren't really values, they're just marketing words."

I scanned the board for a few minutes, considering each word carefully.

Integrity
Collaboration
Conscientious
Guiding Clients
Teamwork
Growth-oriented
Responsive
Respect
Unity
Golden Rule: Treat others how you want to be treated

We went through each of the 10 remaining words and discussed why each was or was not the perfect value for me and my team.

When I had erased all but three values, I shouted out "RUG! It spells rug!" It was perfect.

A rug pulls a home together, it makes a space personal and comfortable. I also happen to love acronyms.

Respect. Unity. Golden Rule. RUG. I could hardly breathe, I was so excited! Out of 500 words, I was certain divine intervention helped me find those three perfect values.

From that point on, when deciding what to do, we ran everything through those RUG values. Whether it was developing our brand and business structure, or deciding whether or not to add a team member or take on a client, we made sure it passed muster with our values.

Was it respectful of the people involved? Is it the best thing for the team, for unity? And is it treating everyone involved better than we would expect to be treated ourselves, with no expectation of anything in return?

There's not a single person who crosses our path who doesn't remember our values. That's because it's just three simple things. It's not five, or seven, or ten... just *three*. Short, truthful, and to the point.

We don't display the RUG values on some sort of motivational poster, either. Those values reside in our hearts and minds where real values should.

Another part of branding is figuring out *why* you do what you do. So of course, during one of our interviews Brad asked why I did real estate.

"Because I love it, and it pays the bills."

"What if you won the lottery and didn't need the money? Would you just walk in one day and say 'see ya, I just won the lottery'?"

"*No.*" I had a strong gut reaction; it was like my whole body rejected the idea of giving up on my work, on my team.

"I wouldn't quit like that for a couple reasons. Number one, I wouldn't do that to other people. I feel responsible for helping them be successful, and for their livelihood. Number two, which may make me a bad business-person, is I would keep on working just because I love doing it, I love helping people, I love helping them find their nest. To me, that's a big deal. And I need to do something meaningful in my life, not just have a bunch of money in the bank."

That led us to a clear vision for what we wanted our brand to focus on – enriching life transitions. This was nothing new, but now we had put it into words. For 10 years, our team had focused on the life transitions associated with our client's move, but we had never shared that publicly.

Everyone who is buying or selling a home has a story. Buying or selling a house is a huge transition, no matter the catalyst, and we want to be there as a supportive guide during our client's journey.

If the reason for moving is joyous like a wedding, a birth, or an adoption, we want to make it that much better.

If the purpose of moving is sad, like a death, illness, or job loss, we want to help make the process less painful.

Enriching life transitions would be our stated vision.

This vision fit perfectly with our value proposition, which is the unique thing our team could offer to clients over-and-above just being real estate agents. Our team made a point to understand each client's unique story, apply relevant insights, and craft a custom solution.

Everything we talked about during the branding process was about the life journey, the path of our clients, and ourselves. Path was the one word that kept coming up in our meetings, and I was sure I wanted "path" to be part of the new brand name.

In the middle of the branding process in 2013, my husband David and I found time to go on vacation to the beach. I didn't know at the time that Brad would be working on the name while I was gone. He took a deep dive and put together a whole brand name presentation.

He used examples like "Garden & Gun" and "Crate & Barrel." He pointed to the ampersand as a creative and collaborative symbol. Ampersands connect things, like connecting people with homes. He knew I appreciated alliteration, balance, and symmetry, and suggested the word "post."

Real estate signs are *posts* in the ground. We help clients by guiding them along their *path*. It was perfect.

Path & Post

As soon as I heard the name, I was sold. It would cost $2,400 to buy the URL for pathpost.com.

Brad suggested I think on the name and talk to David about it before purchasing the website domain, but my gut said it was time to jump. Before I even left that meeting with Brad, I pulled out my credit card and purchased the URL right then and there.

We checked for federal trademarks, and we were clear. It was full speed ahead.

Once we settled on our brand name, we got to work on our image. We collaborated with a well-known local designer to create a one of a kind ampersand. The ampersand we picked had straight and curved accents, to represent both straight and curved paths.

We decided to use all lowercase letters in our logo, so it was friendly and approachable, and we chose the color blue since it stands for navigation and connections (social media companies and navigation applications often use blue in their logos). Blue, from a branding standpoint, is also known to represent trust.

As soon as we saw the Path & Post logo and design elements all together, I was in love with it. It was different, clean, friendly, and honest. It felt innovative, but comfortable.

The words had meaning and the design felt right.

Just 90 days from when Brad started working with me, we introduced our new brand to the team.

When everyone heard "Path & Post" would be the new team name, they were worried about the potential consequences of taking my name out of the brand, because everyone always called asking for me. They felt like the brand *was* me. There was nervousness, understandably. Would this hurt our business?

I assured them that our team had always been a collective effort and was never about me. Our rebranding was simply meant to share that reality with the public, our clients. It would be a challenging transition, but worth it in the end.

Things were moving quickly, and I was so grateful that my team stuck with me through that uncertain time. I remember Lisa Millsap, the first person to join my team, saying "I've been with you for 10 years Becky, and you've never led us astray. I trust you to lead us." She's always been my best cheerleader on the team, and I can't possibly explain how valuable her support and friendship has been.

For the first time in 10 years, everyone on the team got new, matching email addresses that day, ending in "@pathpost.com." We handed out gift bags with branded pens and coffee mugs, and everyone got new business cards. We wanted to make it fun and exciting. The website and brand would launch Nov. 12, 2013… 11-12-13. This was our new beginning.

Takeaways:
- Leadership requires big decisions: trust your intuition
- Your brand is the unique essence of your business

11 11-12-13

The much anticipated day came and we launched the Path & Post brand. For us, customization was key.

The top banners of most real estate websites all look similar. Agents and brokers often rely on cookie cutter templates, with only the photo and contact information customized. Many agents focus on self-promotion instead of making it about the client.

We aimed to be more authentic, more friendly, more approachable. We wanted to create a unique customer experience.

Instead of focusing on the real estate agents, we wanted to focus on what we offer customers and what makes us different. We took photos of ourselves off the front page of our website, and we designed our home page to be more useful for consumers.

Instead of focusing purely on transactions like many in the industry were trained to do, we focused on our client's life transition. Transitions over transactions.

The brand launch was met with excitement and support from our broker David Moody, and our colleagues at ERA Sunrise Realty.

A few weeks after the brand launch, our team won all the top awards in the U.S. for ERA Franchise Systems – it was a clean sweep. We were No. 1 in sales and No. 1 in customer service among more than 30,000 ERA agents in the country.

We were at the pinnacle of success... and we had just decided to change everything, even our name. Those were the last awards we earned as The Becky Babcock Team; now, we would move forward as the Path & Post Team.

Some people thought I was crazy, but I knew we were headed in the right direction and the team trusted me to lead them on this new path.

In the first few years after the rebranding, our workflow was perfected and streamlined. We had more time, less frustration, and more business than ever. For the first time in years, I was able to spend as much time with my family as I wanted: we went on family vacations, enjoyed regular family dinners, and welcomed our first six grandchildren into the family.

Before Brad joined me, I rarely had time to step back and look at the big picture, because I was too busy frantically keeping our team moving. Now, I had time to plan and lead the team like never before.

Imagine you're in a canoe and it's filling with water, and you have a small plastic cup to bail water out as quickly as possible. Imagine the water is pouring in faster than you can get it out of the canoe. Because you're so fixated on using this little cup to bail out water, you never have the chance to stand up and survey the canoe as a whole.

Then along comes someone who gives you a big bucket, and you can now bail water out of your leaking canoe faster than it's pouring in. So you manage to get ahead of the leak. You stand up, only to realize that there's a cork behind you, just the same size as the hole in your canoe. Because of this new perspective, you learn how to drastically improve your situation and stop your canoe from sinking, all with a whole lot less effort and wasted work.

But, until you were able to get a wider perspective, you couldn't have seen the solution.

Brad brought me that bucket and helped me step back for the first time in a decade to see where the holes were. And together, we plugged them. Since we fixed the leaks, we could start to build a stronger and better boat for the long journey onward.

Being able to step back and look at the team as a whole helped me realize some important things. Up to this point, the Path & Post Team, and previously The Becky Babcock Team, had operated under the ERA Sunrise Realty brokerage.

We loved our broker, but, along with the ERA franchise and the Sunrise Realty brokerage came certain branding limitations, due to state law and franchise guidelines. It wasn't anything personal, but it presented several challenges.

When it came to branding, we ran into problems. Since our signs, websites, and marketing material all had to show both "ERA Sunrise Realty" and our team name, "Path & Post," we were limited in our marketing and brand design.

We had to keep our brand colors as basic blue and charcoal to be balanced with the ERA brand colors, while also trying to differentiate the two.

It also got confusing for customers who would mistake our team brand for a brokerage of its own – a problem nobody saw coming. One time someone was looking for my team office and couldn't find it, so they stopped at the ERA office to ask if they knew where Path & Post was, only to be told it was just an office within the ERA office.

From the late-2013 launch, through 2016, the Path & Post brand kept growing, and people started asking why my team was still part of a different company, instead of opening its own brokerage.

I didn't intend for our team to outgrow ERA, but Path & Post was becoming its own entity.

After a couple years as the Path & Post Team at ERA Sunrise Realty, it became clear that eventually, and soon, Path & Post would need to become its own brokerage. Having those three years to catch my breath and think bigger, I realized the inherent problems of being co-branded with a large real estate brokerage. We realized our brand was our value, so we couldn't continue growing successfully unless our brand became its own independent brokerage.

Being independent would give us the maximum freedom and opportunities to grow our brand and help clients find their path.

I have always been a loyal person, so I struggled with the conviction that Path & Post would eventually need to break free. But, I knew my brand couldn't grow to its full potential as long as we stayed co-branded with ERA.

Takeaways:
- Transitions over transactions
- Processes and systems must be scalable to grow
- Branding is about the client experience

12 CUSTOMIZE FOR CLIENT EXPERIENCES

Before we could think about opening our own brokerage, I needed to take an even further step back from working with clients, in order to focus on a plan for our team's future. That meant I had to start handing more clients off to our team's buyer and seller specialists.

My method of handing off clients to team members was to sit down with the client and the other agent in a meeting where I'd introduce them to each other. This personal touch worked exceptionally well.

Here's an example of what I might say during a meeting where I introduce a client to one of my team specialists, and why:

"Hi Bill and Mary, I'm Becky, and this is our team seller specialist. We're business partners."

I always refer to each person on the team as a business partner. They don't work *for* me, we're partners. I acknowledge my team member's expertise, so the clients know they're in good hands.

"This is my business partner. She's been licensed for 14 years, was actually the No. 1 agent at her office before we partnered up."

Each agent on the team has their own unique areas of expertise, and I try to point those out to our clients. I also like to mention how I have my own family and friends work with our team's specialists, because I trust them to do an exceptional job.

"Now, she is in charge of managing and marketing listings, follow-up, and negotiations, so she will be your primary point of contact after today. My primary role is in the background, where I'll work on processes, systems, marketing, and covering team members who are out sick or on vacation. That way we won't drop any balls for you, does that make sense?"

The client is always ecstatic to be working with someone so skilled. It's all about emphasizing each agent's strengths, and matching those strengths with a client's needs.

Each team member gets their own custom introduction that focuses on their expertise.

Another one of our team's seller specialist, for example, has a much different background than the previous one. I'll sometimes introduce her like this:

"This is our seller specialist, and she has been licensed since 2000. She earned her business degree from UGA. When I recruited her to work for my team, she had a background in new homes and builder analytics and was working for 150 builder clients at one time, managing what type of home features, lots, and marketing would maximize sales."

I like to use words like 'recruited' and 'sought out,' because it shows clients that I was seeking out the specialist's talent to add to my team.

"She is awesome, and when we walk through your house today, she's going to be able to tell you exactly what to do to sell, because she knows what buyers want and what they'll pay for. That's a skill set you don't get very often in real estate, but because of her background you get that advantage. She does residential resale, working as my business partner."

Then during the walkthrough I let that seller specialist lead the dialogue because that helps build trust.

Before choosing a buyer or seller specialist, we always try to determine the client's personality and decide on the best way to work with them. Some people want to know every detail of what their agent is doing, while others would rather sit back and hear from their agent only when there's an offer. Clients' needs vary widely, so getting an idea of what they expect helps us deliver the service they want.

Our entire team uses the BOLT System for understanding four general personalities, developed in 1968 by Charles Clarke Consulting. It's similar to DISC profiles, which are commonly used to describe personality types in a business setting, but in my opinion the BOLT System is easier and more fun to apply on a day-to-day basis.

It goes like this: the four main categories of the BOLT System are Bulls, Owls, Lambs, and Tigers. In general, bulls like control and want to know the bottom line upfront; owls are all about logic and want to know the details; lambs don't like conflict and prefer to move slower than other personality types; and tigers are usually outgoing and spontaneous. Of course, there's much more detail to each category, but this gives an idea of what each type is like.

Most people have aspects of more than one of the four categories in their personality, and this system helps our team to maximize the benefit of each interaction with our clients.

Knowing what personality type we are working with lets us focus on what our clients want, rather than using a one-size-fits-all approach, which is typical in our industry.

It all goes back to our value proposition of learning our client's story, applying relevant insights, and creating a custom solution to meet their needs.

So whoever initially interacts with a new client, whether it's an administrator who answered a call at the office, or someone who got a lead from our website, we always try to pinpoint the personality type of our clients.

The client may be an owl who wants to know the ins and outs of how their listing will be handled, or they may be a lamb who wants more guidance and support through the emotional part of moving.

For example, say we have an owl. I will send the client to a seller specialist and suggest they guide the client by presenting facts and figures, because the owl client needs to know that their agent can handle their need for detail. If I'm at the agent's presentation,

I might complement it by asking a question about the market, which isn't rehearsed but I'm confident my team member can answer. That would show the owl client that their agent is at the top of their game and prepared to handle any needs that might arise.

If we know the client's background and what they're looking for, we can hand-pick which specialist is best for them to work with. Our team members know each other well enough to be able to do that, too.

Once we had perfected the art of matching clients to specialists, I was able to refocus my attention on our company's transition to becoming an independent brokerage.

Takeaways:
- Treat team members as business partners, not employees
- Customizing the client's experience is key to success
- Learn to step back and plan for the future

13 CORE VALUES

Naysayers warned our rebranding from the Becky Babcock Team to the Path & Post Team in 2013 was risky – but, the next three years solidified our decision. By 2016, we had been the No. 1 agent team for ERA in the U.S. for three years in a row, while also earning the top award in customer service. We were on track to be No. 1 for the fourth consecutive year.

Despite our success, there were inherent limitations being co-branded with a national franchise. So in mid-2016, Brad and I began discussing the possibility of opening an independent brokerage. For months we worked out whether or not it would be possible: could we afford our own office space; did we want to manage our own brokerage; would we be able to maintain or improve our team members' income? By fall, we made the decision to launch an independent brokerage later that year.

Being the No. 1 agent team in the U.S. for ERA, I knew leaving our old brokerage to open a new company could hurt our broker: not just financially, but from typical industry gossip.

Our broker had been great to us, both professionally and personally, so we took an unconventional approach to leaving – one that would benefit both our new company and our old broker.

First, I asked my team members out to lunch for a special meeting where I shared the decision to leave ERA and open an independent brokerage. As soon as I announced the news, the room filled with enthusiastic applause. I was expecting shock or concern, but my team's collective response was, "what took you so long?"

Then, I spoke to my broker in private so we could prepare for the transition together. I was able to give him two months notice and he agreed to keep the move a secret until the public announcement. We worked together to plan a smooth departure.

On the day of the announcement, I headed-off any potential gossip by addressing my broker in an open letter on the Path & Post website. In the letter, I thanked him for 13 great years of working together, and explained why opening an independent brokerage was the next step for my growing team.

My letter and the gratitude I expressed within was sincere. We posted a link to the letter on the Path & Post social media sites and the post was shared and commented on by industry leaders, brokers, the CEO and President of ERA Franchise Systems, and my old broker himself, who responded with his own public letter of support.

The transition couldn't have been any smoother. Even after we opened our new brokerage, our old broker invited the entire team back for the ERA Sunrise Realty Christmas party, which we joyfully attended.

The unconventional approach we took in opening our own brokerage aligned with our core values, and allowed us to maintain our relationships with friends at our old brokerage. It also made waves in the industry; we set a new standard for open and honest communication between brokers and agent teams.

We received calls and messages from other agents and brokers from across the country, commenting on how respectfully we handled the transition. That meant the world to me, because it was confirmation we lived our core values when we came to a critical crossroad.

I've always been a trailblazer; cutting my own path in life. I may not always be able to see beyond the next bend, but I've learned that whenever I trust my intuition and move forward with respect, unity, and the desire to treat others the way I want to be treated, I always end up on a meaningful path.

AFTERWARD: PATH & POST

Soon after opening the brokerage, we expanded on the core residential team, adding a new homes division and a commercial division. The growth we experienced in our first year was confirmation of our decision to open an independent brokerage.

Our team model continues to be our key to success, with everyone at the company working together for the same clients, instead of competing with each other like in a traditional real estate brokerage model. Path & Post's collaborative team structure and our freedom as an independent brokerage enable us to create memorable experiences for clients and meaningful work for our team members.

In 2017, Path & Post was named one of America's Best Real Estate Teams by REAL Trends.

People often ask me to share the key to Path & Post's success. I hope by sharing how I found my path, you're inspired and motivated you to find yours! Here are my 10 best nuggets of advice:

Be True To Yourself

You can't create a fake persona because it sounds good. Be the real you. Know WHY you do what you do. Watch Simon Sinek's WHY video.

Know & Live By Your Core Values

Leading with core values like RUG (Respect, Unity, Golden Rule) gives me a good lens to use for making decisions. Your business values and personal values are identical if they are real.

Lead By Serving Others

No one thrives in an atmosphere of top down, heavy handed, fear based management. Servant leaders show empathy and support, focusing on human relationships. Leading by example works in life and in business.

Part of leading is being generous by giving back to your community, your place of worship, humanitarian organizations, and even the random stranger who crosses your path and needs help.

Be Open To Change

Change can stop you in your tracks, or motivate you; refusing to adapt as the world changes leads to demise. Technology innovation as well as human experiences are constantly moving and evolving, so standing still will leave you behind.

Watch Out For Shiny Objects

There is no magic tool or silver bullet for business success. Chasing shiny objects can distract you. They waste your time and money. Instead, spend quality time and energy building your business.

Your Grandmother Was Right

Good old fashioned hard work makes things happen. There is no shortcut. Put in the effort it takes to get the results you want.

Don't Be A Copycat

Don't try to be like me. Be you. Every human has their own unique value. Get ideas from others, then create your own business system that fits your style.

Stay Off Pedestals

There is a fine line between sharing your competency and track record versus looking like an egomaniac. Even worse, don't stretch the truth about your track record. Too many agents brag about being #1 when reading between the lines shows they are fake. Be honest.

Listen To Your Gut

God gives us the gift of intuition. If your gut is talking, you should listen.

Don't Let Urgent Things Wipe Important Things Off Your Radar

Putting out the daily fires in business is urgent. But what matters most in life, like your family, friends, and health, are important. I like to say, "There is no real estate emergency other than a house on fire!" So never miss your kid's ball game or time with special people. Real estate can wait a few hours.

ABOUT THE AUTHOR

Becky's 20-plus years of real estate experience began with her entry into the industry as a solo agent at the age of 22. Over the course of her career, Becky evolved into leading her own award-winning team, earning numerous national, state, and local awards in sales and customer service.

The Path & Post team has ranked among the top real estate teams in Georgia and the U.S., and was the No. 1 agent team in sales in the U.S. for a national franchise, as well as the No. 1 team in customer service based on actual customer surveys after closings. The team now operates as an independent brokerage to provide maximum freedom, opportunity, and benefits to clients and team members.

Becky leads her team with passion and vision in an authentic, down-to-earth way. Her leadership goes beyond the routine industry topics, with a greater focus on the influence of relationships, trust, and personality styles in business and how those personality types influence sales dynamics.

    Becky's areas of expertise include the importance of core values, leading so others want to follow, delivering a branded experience, building a collaborative team, utilizing technology tools for efficiency and optimal service, social media marketing and engagement, lead conversion strategies in a competitive market, growth strategies to get to the next level, creative problem solving, and personality-based selling to better serve clients.

Made in the USA
Columbia, SC
25 April 2018